UNKIN
UNICOᴿNS

For Alicia 17:6:23.
Gp.X.

UNKIND TO UNICORNS

COMIC VERSE OF
A. E. HOUSMAN

EDITED BY
ARCHIE BURNETT

SELECTED BY
J. ROY BIRCH

WITH AN INTRODUCTION BY
NORMAN PAGE

ILLUSTRATIONS BY
DAVID HARRIS

THE HOUSMAN SOCIETY

First published in Great Britain in 1995
by Silent Books Ltd and The Housman Society

Second edition 1999 published by
The Housman Society
80 New Road, Bromsgrove, Worcestershire, B60 2LA

© The Housman Society 1999
© Text and notes copyright Archie Burnett 1999
© Illustrations copyright David Harris 1999

No part of this book may be reproduced in any form or by any means
without prior permission in writing from the publisher.

ISBN 0 904579 15 8

British Library Cataloguing-in-Publication Data.
A catalogue record for this book is available from the British Library.

Typeset by Textype Typesetters, Cambridge
Printed in Great Britain by St Edmundsbury Press Ltd
Bury St Edmunds, Suffolk

EDITOR'S PREFACE

When the first edition of this selection of Housman's comic verse by Roy Birch appeared in 1995, it was the largest since that published in Laurence Housman's *A. E. H.* in 1937. Like all previous selections and editions of Housman's poetry, it was superseded at the end of 1997 by the Oxford English Texts edition of *The Poems of A. E. Housman*, published by Oxford University Press. The existence of a comprehensive scholarly edition does not mean that there is now no place for an illustrated selection of the comic verse, however: the readership addressed and the function fulfilled are altogether different.

The predominant aim of this second edition has been to correct the errors in the text of the first. Roy Birch's selection has been kept, as has Norman Page's brief introduction. In view of the extensive commentary in the Oxford edition, the notes at the back of this volume now provide only brief information on the sources of the texts.

INTRODUCTION

"He had," said Housman's brother Laurence after his death, "about the happiest *laugh* I ever heard, ringing and bell-like." His "saving grace", Laurence added, was "his keen sense of humour". The notion of a laughing Housman may not find ready acceptance, so firmly entrenched is the legend of the curmudgeonly recluse who engaged in acrimonious disputes over minute points of classical learning. Like most legends, this one contains a fair amount of truth. But legends also tend to simplify the complex human reality, and there is abundant evidence that Housman, severe scholar and poet of nostalgic sentiment, also relished a joke and was often the cause of a similar relish in others.

Until a great change was wrought by his mother's death on his twelfth birthday, he grew up in a happy Victorian household in which the family very largely made their own entertainment, and this must often have taken the form of skits, parodies and word-games. Lewis Carroll's *Alice's Adventures in Wonderland* and C. S. Calverley's *Verses and Translations* both appeared during Housman's childhood years and serve to remind us that Victorian earnestness was only one aspect of a many-sided culture that also witnessed the golden age of nonsense and limericks, parodies and puns.

Later he earned a reputation as an outstanding after-dinner speaker and raconteur, and his letters include many examples of polished wit. Some of his epigrams, indeed, have a distinctly Wildean flavour - and it was, after all, during the Nineties that he emerged both as a poet and as a professional scholar. Even his scholarly prefaces and reviews, though primarily concerned with technical matters, contain some brilliantly and exuberantly witty passages. He enjoyed telling and listening to jokes and comic anecdotes, and did not object if they were obscene. And on his deathbed he mustered enough strength to chuckle at a funny (and faintly indelicate) story told him by his doctor, and to make a jest in return.

All of this makes it less surprising that Housman should have been a fertile and accomplished comic versifier, and the material collected in this volume exhibits various aspects of his comic art. He excels as a parodist, and his send-up of Longfellow in *The shades of night were falling fast* and of the robust hymnody of the Salvation Army in *"Hallelujah!" was the only observation* seem to me to stand comparison with the best of Carroll or Calverley. *The Elephant, Infant Innocence,* and other examples are closer to the vein of nonsense mined by Edward Lear. Particularly characteristic is the mock-solemn manner of a poem such as *It is a fearful thing to be/The Pope.* Some items show an ability to write in the vein of other comic masters: *Inhuman Henry,* for instance, could have found a place in Belloc's *Cautionary Verses,* and *Infant Innocence* in Harry Graham's *Ruthless Rhymes.*

Housman belongs, in other words, to the great tradition of Victorian and early twentieth-century comic verse, a distinctly irreverent alternative to the more solemn great tradition of Tennyson and others. Comedy too can have its serious side, and the work of Housman and others can be seen as subversive, not only holding up to ridicule such elocutionary warhorses as Longfellow's *Excelsior* but undermining orthodox Victorian ideas concerning the family and, particularly, the child. The children depicted in the poems of Housman, the 'confirmed bachelor' (in the phrase of his generation), are much closer to those in the stories of Saki than to the little angels of Dickens or Mrs Henry Wood.

One recalls that, asked to make a speech at the wedding of one of his relatives, Housman told a story of a certain African tribe that was accustomed on such occasions to cook and eat the mothers-in-law. The same spirit of mischievous and iconoclastic fun infects the comic poems. At the same time they are highly accomplished specimens of verse-writing whose catchy and complex rhythms probably owed something to the music-hall as well as to traditions of written verse. A piece such as *The Amphisbæna* accommodates mock-solemn language in a jaunty verse-form, and the result is as accomplished and as satisfying in its way as any of the serious poems for which Housman is much better known. The present volume should help to win him the place he richly deserves among the masters of comic verse in English.

NORMAN PAGE

9

The shades of night were falling fast,
    And the rain was falling faster,
When through an Alpine village passed
    An Alpine village pastor:
A youth who bore mid snow and ice
    A bird that wouldn't chirrup,
And a banner with the strange device -
    "Mrs. Winslow's soothing syrup."

"Beware the pass," the old man said,
    "My bold, my desperate fellah;
Dark lowers the tempest overhead,
    And you'll want your umberella;
And the roaring torrent is deep and wide -
    You may hear how loud it washes."
But still that clarion voice replied:
    "I've got my old goloshes."

"Oh, stay," the maiden said, "and rest
    (For the wind blows from the nor'ward)
Thy weary head upon my breast -
    And please don't think I'm forward."
A tear stood in his bright blue eye,
    And he gladly would have tarried;
But still he answered with a sigh:
    "Unhappily I'm married."

THE CROCODILE

OR PUBLIC DECENCY

Though some at my aversion smile,
I cannot love the crocodile.
Its conduct does not seem to me
Consistent with sincerity.

   Where Nile, with beneficial flood,
Improves the desert sand to mud,
The infant child, its banks upon,
Will run about with nothing on.
The London County Council not
Being adjacent to the spot,
This is the consequence. Meanwhile,
What is that object in the Nile
Which swallows water, chokes and spits?
It is the crocodile in fits.

"Oh infant! oh my country's shame!
Suppose a European came!
Picture his feelings, on his pure
Personally conducted tour!
The British Peer's averted look,
The mantling blush of Messrs. Cook!
Come, awful infant, come and be
Dressed, if in nothing else, in me."

Then disappears into the Nile
The infant, clad in crocodile,
And meekly yields his youthful breath
To darkness, decency, and death.
His mother, in the local dells,
Deplores him with Egyptian yells:
Her hieroglyphic howls are vain,
Nor will the lost return again.
The crocodile itself no less
Displays, but does not feel, distress,
And with its tears augments the Nile;
The false, amphibious crocodile.

"Is it that winds Etesian blow,
Or melts on Ethiop hills the snow?"
So, midst the inundated scene,
Enquire the floating fellaheen.
From Cairo's ramparts gazing far
The mild Khedive and stern Sirdar
Say, as they scan the watery plain,
"There goes that crocodile again."
The copious tribute of its lids
Submerges half the pyramids,
And over all the Sphinx it flows,
Except her non-existent nose.

Amelia mixed the mustard,
    She mixed it good and thick;
She put it in the custard
    And made her mother sick;
And showing satisfaction
    By many a loud huzza
"Observe" said she "the action
    Of mustard on mamma."

What, little Arthur, do you know
Of Marcus Tullius Cicero?
He wrote about a nasty brute,
A Frenchman called De Senectute.

Who, Arthur, was Horatius Flaccus?
He was a votary of Bacchus.
And who was Festus Avienus?
He was a votary of Venus.
Of whom was Decius Mus a votary?
He was a member of a coterie.

———————

What was the date of Volcacius Sedigitus?
    What might the date of that good man be?
We will not allow such a detail to fidget us:
    Put him B.C. if he wasn't A.D.
The annals of Rome are sufficiently spacious
For even Voldigitus Thingamycacius.

15

It is a fearful thing to be
   The Pope.
That cross will not be laid on me,
   I hope.
A righteous God would not permit
   It.
The Pope himself must often say,
After the labours of the day,
"It is a fearful thing to be
   Me."

THOMASINA AND THE AMPHISBÆNA
OR HORRORS OF HORTICULTURE

"In the back, back garden, Thomasina,
  Did you recently vociferate a squeal?"
"Oh, I trod upon an amphisbæna,
  And it bit me on the toe and on the heel.
    Yes, it bit me (do you know?)
    With its tail upon the toe
While it bit me with its head upon the heel."

"How excessively distracting and confusing.
  Pray, what, Thomasina, did you do?"
"Oh, I took the garden scissors I was using
  And I snipped it irretrievably in two.
    And it split with such a scrunch
    That I shall not want my lunch,
And if you had heard the noise, no more would you."

"And where, Thomasina, are the sections
  Of the foe that you courageously repressed?"
"Oh, they ran away in opposite directions
  And they vanished in the east and in the west.
    And the way they made me squint,
    It would melt a heart of flint,
And I think that I will go upstairs and rest."

THE ELEPHANT
OR THE FORCE OF HABIT

A tail behind, a trunk in front,
Complete the usual elephant.
The tail in front, the trunk behind,
Is what you very seldom find.

If you for specimens should hunt
With trunks behind and tails in front,
That hunt would occupy you long;
The force of habit is so strong.

THE CAT
OR IRRELEVANT INFORMATION

The Cat, in hopes of catching larks,
    Leaps high into the air;
To dive into the sea for sharks
    She does not seem to care;
The Cat was one of Noah's Ark's
Inhabitants; she never barks;
Her back is said to give out sparks
In thunderstorms; - but these remarks
    Are neither here nor there.

INFANT INNOCENCE

The Grizzly Bear is huge and wild;
He has devoured the infant child.
The infant child is not aware
He has been eaten by the bear.

────────

There is Hallelujah Hannah
    Walking backwards down the lane,
And I hear the loud Hosanna
    Of regenerated Jane;
And Lieutenant Isabella
    In the centre of them comes,
Dealing blows with her umbrella
    On the trumpets and the drums.

────────

"Hallelujah!" was the only observation
    That escaped Lieutenant-Colonel Mary-Jane,
When she tumbled off the platform in the station
    And was cut in little pieces by the train;
    Mary-Jane, the train is through ye,
    Hallelujah! Hallelujah!
We will gather up the fragments that remain.

Elegant Edith and Modest Minnie
A-walking along by the side of a spinney.

Modest Minnie in front proceedeth,
And close behind trots elegant Edith.

When out of the spinney a midge arises
And taketh and biteth the two Miss Wises.

"Oh something has just come out of the spinney
And taken and bitten me, modest Minnie."

"Oh elegant Edith, you need not squall so,
For something has taken and bitten me also."

"O modest Minnie, by what are we bitten?
A tortoiseshell cat or a tabby kitten?

What animal is it whose venom rankles
In both our modest and elegant ankles?

A mouse, or a midge that lives in the spinney,
Or a cow or a crocodile, modest Minnie?"

"Oh elegant Edith, it does not matter;
Carbolic will do us more good than chatter.

Whatever it is, it's a nasty creature
Whose conduct has no redeeming feature.

For of all odd acts it is quite the oddest
To bite the elegant and the modest."

Here ends the tale of the two Miss Wises.
It might be true if it wasn't lieses.

Oh have you caught the tiger?
  And can you hold him tight?
And what immortal hand or eye
Could frame his fearful symmetry?
  And does he try to bite?

Yes, I have caught the tiger,
  And he was hard to catch.
O tiger, tiger, do not try
To put your tail into my eye,
  And do not bite and scratch.

Yes, I have caught the tiger.
   O tiger, do not bray!
And what immortal hand or eye
Could frame his fearful symmetry
   I should not like to say.

And may I see the tiger?
   I should indeed delight
To see so large an animal
Without a voyage to Bengal.
   And mind you hold him tight.

Yes, you may see the tiger;
   It will amuse you much.
The tiger is, as you will find,
A creature of the feline kind.
   And mind you do not touch.

And do you feed the tiger,
   And do you keep him clean?
He has a less contented look
Than in the Natural History book,
   And seems a trifle lean.

Oh yes, I feed the tiger,
   And soon he will be plump;
I give him groundsel fresh and sweet,
And much canary-seed to eat,
   And wash him at the pump.

It seems to me the tiger
   Has not been lately fed,
Not for a day or two at least;
And that is why the noble beast
   Has bitten off your head.

As I was walking slowly
   Among the grassy hay,
Oh, there I met an old man
   Whose nerves had given way:
His heels were in an ants' nest,
   His head was in a tree,
And his arms went round and round and round,
   And he squealed repeatedly.

I waited very kindly,
   And attended to his wants;
For I put his heels into the tree,
   And his head among the ants:
I tied his hands with a boot-lace,
   And I filled his mouth with hay,
And I said "Good-bye; fine morning:
   Many happy returns of the day!"

He could not squeal distinctly,
   And his arms would not go round;
Yet he did not leave off making
   A discontented sound.
I gazed at him a little while,
   As I walked among the trees,
And I said "When old men's nerves give way,
   How hard they are to please!"

PURPLE WILLIAM
OR THE LIAR'S DOOM

The hideous hue which William is
Was not originally his:
So long as William told the truth
He was a usual-coloured youth.

He now is purple. One fine day
His tender father chanced to say
"What colour is a whelp, and why?"
"Purple" was William's false reply.

"Pooh" said his Pa, "You silly elf,
It's no more purple than yourself.
Dismiss the notion from your head."
"I, too, am purple" William said.

And he *was* purple. With a yell
His mother off the sofa fell
Exclaiming "William's purple! Oh!"
William replied "I told you so."

His parents, who could not support
The pungency of this retort,
Died with a simultaneous groan.
The purple orphan was alone.

The African Lion

To meet a bad lad on the African waste
    Is a thing that a lion enjoys;
But he rightly and strongly objects to the taste
    Of good and uneatable boys.

When he bites off a piece of a boy of that sort
    He spits it right out of his mouth,
And retires with a loud and dissatisfied snort
    To the east, or the west, or the south.

So lads of good habits, on coming across
    A lion, need feel no alarm,
For they know they are sure to escape with the loss
    Of a leg, or a head, or an arm.

Now all day the hornèd herds
Dance to the piping of the birds;
Now the bumble-bee is rife,
And other forms of insect life;
The skylark in the sky so blue
Now makes noise enough for two,
And lovers on the grass so green
- Muse, oh Muse, eschew th'obscene.

Aunts and Nieces
or Time and Space

Some nieces won't, some nieces can't
Imbibe instruction from an aunt.
Eliza scorned her good Aunt Clare.
Where is Eliza now? Ah, where?

   "Avoid, at the approach of dark,
Eliza, the umbrageous park.
During the daytime, lairs and dens
Conceal its direr denizens.
But when that brilliant orb, the Sun,
His useful journey nearly done,
Approaches the horizon's verge,
They will, my dearest niece, emerge;
And forth the cockatrice will frisk,
And out will bounce the basilisk,
And the astoundingly absurd
Yet dangerous cockyoly-bird
Will knock you, with its baneful beak,
Into the middle of next week."

   "Pooh," said Eliza, "that it can't.
Still, if you think so, thank you, Aunt.
Now, after this exhausting talk,
I think that I will take a walk."

   She therefore fetched her parasol,
Her gloves and reticule and all,
And need I specify the spot
Which drew her footsteps? I need not.

"Eliza," said her aunt, "is late.
Jane, place the crumpets by the grate.
What was that distant crow I heard?
Was it the cockyoly-bird?
I think so. There it goes again.
You may remove the crumpets, Jane."

　　Meanwhile Eliza took the air.
(Shall I? – I will not – mention where),
And as the afternoon progressed
She sat upon the grass to rest,
Drew from her reticule a bun,
And bit it in the setting sun.
Soon, with her mouth full, she perceives
Movements and rustlings in the leaves
Which spoil the situation's charm
And tend to substitute alarm.
She dropped the bun and said "Dear me!
I fear I shall be late for tea."
Then, from behind, a vicious peck
Descended on Eliza's neck.
Eliza into the azure distance
Followed the line of least resistance.

In the middle of next week
There will be heard a piercing shriek,
And looking pale and weak and thin
Eliza will come flying in.

The Latin author Lucan,
When bitten by a toucan,
   Exclaimed in anguish "O!
That bird must have been frantic
To cross the broad Atlantic
   From distant Mexico,
And come to ancient Rome,
And bite me in my home,
And make me cry in anguish
And in the Latin language
O!"

———

Little Miss Muffet sat on a tuffet
Opening her mouth very wide.
There came a great spider; she opened it wider;
And the spider ran down her inside.

FRAGMENT OF AN
ENGLISH OPERA

(designed as a model for young librettists.)

Dramatis personae: Father (bass), Mother (contralto),
Daughter (soprano).

Scene: a Room. *Time*: Evening.

Fath.	Retire, my daughter;
	Prayers have been said:
	Take your warm water
	And go to bed.
Daught.	But I had rather
	Sit up instead.
Fath.	I am your father,
	So go to bed.
Daught.	Are you my father?
Fath.	I think so, rather:
	You go to bed.
Moth.	My daughter, vanish;
	You hear me speak:
	This is not Spanish,
	Nor is it Greek.
Daught.	Oh, what a bother!
	Would I were dead!
Moth.	I am your mother,
	So go to bed.
Daught.	Are you my mother?
Moth.	You have no other:
	You go to bed.

Fath.	Take your bed-candle And take it quick. This is the handle.
Daught.	Is *this* the handle?

Fath.	No, that's the wick.
	This is the handle,
	   At this end here.
	Take your bed-candle
	   And disappear.

Daught.	Oh dear, oh dear!

F. and M.	Take your warm water,
	   As we have said;
	You are our daughter,
	   So go to bed.

Daught.	Am I your daughter?
F. and M.	If not, you oughter: You go to bed.

Daught.	I am their daughter;
	If not, I oughter:
	   Prayers have been said.
	This is my mother;
	I have no other:
	   Would I were dead!
	That is my father;
	He thinks so, rather:
	   Oh dear, oh dear!
	I take my candle;
	This is the handle:
	   I disappear.

F. and M.	The coast is clear.

WHIT-MONDAY, 1903

How lovely the band and how lovely the banners!
How lovely the kids with their company manners!
   How lovely the lovely balloon!
How lovely the cups of the Chinaman's nectar!
How lovely the lawn and how lovely the rector!
   How equally lovely the moon!

How lovely the skips of the skippers a-skipping!
How lovely the slips of the slippers a-slipping!
   How lovely, how lovely indeed!
How lovely the strains that my pen is inditing!
There's nothing so easy as meaningless writing;
   'Tis only a trouble to read.

———————

The oyster is found in the ocean
   And cucumbers grow on the land;
And the oyster is slightly the moister,
   As most people well understand.

And the reason I mentioned this fact was
   That oyster and moister will rhyme;
And *cucumber*, that word exact was
   The noun to be brought in this time.

And therefore with joy the most boister'us
   I conclude with the prudent remark,
That as to the whiskers of oysters
   I am totally all in the dark.

At the door of my own little hovel,
Reading a novel I sat;
And as I was reading the novel
A gnat flew away with my hat.
As fast as a fraudulent banker
Away with my hat it fled,
And calmly came to an anchor
In the midst of the cucumber-bed.

I went and purchased a yacht,
And traversed the garden-tank,
And I gave it that insect hot
When I got to the other bank;
Of its life I made an abridgment
By squeezing it somewhat flat,
And I cannot think what that midge meant
By flying away with my hat.

Of old the little Busy Bee
  Improved the shining hour,
And gathered honey all the day
  From every opening flower.
But now the little Spelling Bee
  Has new ideas quite,
Gathers, not honey in the day,
  But money in the night.

———————

Oft when the night is chilly
  And creation is ill at ease,
The piano twangles shrilly
  As the cat walks over the keys.
And I lie on my bed complaining,
  "There is nothing at all in that,
'Twould be far more entertaining
  If the keys walked over the cat."

Oft when the night is murky
  I lie on my bed and snore,
And the Sultan exclaims in Turkey,
  "They are taking in coals next door!"
But they say, "May your shadow be glorious,
  O Commander of faithful souls!
'Tis that poet of Queen Victoria's.
  He is snoring - not taking in coals."

INHUMAN HENRY
OR CRUELTY TO FABULOUS ANIMALS

Oh would you know why Henry sleeps,
And why his mourning mother weeps,
And why his weeping mother mourns?
He was unkind to unicorns.

No unicorn, with Henry's leave,
Could dance upon the lawn at eve,
Or gore the gardener's boy in spring,
Or do the very slightest thing.

No unicorn could safely roar
And dash its nose against the door,
Nor sit in peace upon the mat
To eat the dog or drink the cat.

Henry would never in the least
Encourage the heraldic beast:
If there were unicorns about
He went and let the lion out.

The lion, leaping from its chain,
And glaring through its tangled mane,
Would stand on end and bark and bound
And bite what unicorns it found.

And when the lion bit a lot
Was Henry sorry? He was not.
What did his jumps betoken? Joy.
He was a bloody-minded boy.

The Unicorn is not a Goose,
And when they saw the lion loose
They grew increasingly aware
That they had better not be there.

And oh, the unicorn is fleet
And spurns the earth with all its feet:
The lion had to snap and snatch
At tips of tails it could not catch.

Returning home, in temper bad,
It met the sanguinary lad,
And clasping Henry with its claws
It took his legs between its jaws.

"Down, lion, down!" said Henry, "Cease!
My legs immediately release."
His formidable feline pet
Made no reply, but only ate.

The last words that were ever said
By Henry's disappearing head,
In accents of indignant scorn,
Were "I am not a unicorn."

And now you know why Henry sleeps,
And why his mother mourns and weeps,
And why she also weeps and mourns;
So now be kind to unicorns.

FRAGMENT OF A GREEK TRAGEDY

Alcmaeon.   Chorus.

Cho. O suitably-attired-in-leather-boots
      Head of a traveller, wherefore seeking whom
      Whence by what way how purposed art thou
          come
      To this well-nightingaled vicinity?
      My object in enquiring is to know.
      But if you happen to be deaf and dumb
      And do not understand a word I say,
      Nod with your hand to signify as much.
Alc. I journeyed hither a Boeotian road.
Cho. Sailing on horseback or with feet for oars?
Alc. Plying by turns my partnership of legs.
Cho. Beneath a shining or a rainy Zeus?
Alc. Mud's sister, not himself, adorns my shoes.
Cho. To learn your name would not displease me
          much.
Alc. Not all that men desire do they obtain.
Cho. Might I then hear at what your presence shoots?
Alc. A shepherd's questioned mouth informed me
          that -
Cho. What? for I know not yet what you will say.
Alc. Nor will you ever, if you interrupt.
Cho. Proceed, and I will hold my speechless tongue.
Alc. - This house was Eriphyla's, no one's else.
Cho. Nor did he shame his throat with hateful lies.
Alc. May I then enter, passing through the door?
Cho. Go, chase into the house a lucky foot.
      And, O my son, be, on the one hand, good,

And do not, on the other hand, be bad;
For that is very much the safest plan.

Alc.   I go into the house with heels and speed.

Chorus.

In speculation   *Strophe.*
I would not willingly acquire a name
    For ill-digested thought,
    But after pondering much
To this conclusion I at last have come:
    Life is uncertain.
    This truth I have written deep
    In my reflective midriff
    On tablets not of wax,
Nor with a pen did I inscribe it there
For many reasons: *Life*, I say, *is not*
    A stranger to uncertainty.
Not from the flight of omen-yelling fowls
    This fact did I discover,
Nor did the Delphic tripod bark it out,
    Nor yet Dodona.
Its native ingenuity sufficed
    My self-taught diaphragm.

    Why should I mention   *Antistrophe.*
The Inachean daughter, loved of Zeus?
    Her whom of old the gods,
    More provident than kind,
Provided with four hoofs, two horns, one tail,
    A gift not asked for,
    And sent her forth to learn
    The unfamiliar science
    Of how to chew the cud.
She therefore, all about the Argive fields,
Went cropping pale green grass and nettle-tops,

44

Nor did they disagree with her.
Yet, howsoe'er nutritious, such repasts
    I do not hanker after.
Never may Cypris for her seat select
    My dappled liver!
Why should I mention Io? Why indeed?
    I have no notion why.

    But now does my boding heart   *Epode.*
    Unhired, unaccompanied, sing
    A strain not meet for the dance.
    Yea, even the palace appears
    To my yoke of circular eyes
    (The right, nor omit I the left)
    Like a slaughterhouse, so to speak,
    Garnished with woolly deaths
    And many shipwrecks of cows.
I therefore in a Cissian strain lament,
    And to the rapid,
Loud, linen-tattering thumps upon my chest
    Resounds in concert
The battering of my unlucky head.

Eriphyla (within). O, I am smitten with a hatchet's jaw;
    And that in deed and not in word alone.
Cho.   I thought I heard a sound within the house
    Unlike the voice of one that jumps for joy.
Eri.   He splits my skull, not in a friendly way,
    Once more: he purposes to kill me dead.
Cho.   I would not be reputed rash, but yet
    I doubt if all be gay within the house.
Eri.   O! O! another stroke! That makes the third.
    He stabs me to the heart against my wish.
Cho.   If that be so, thy state of health is poor;
    But thine arithmetic is quite correct.

NOTES

Unless it is stated otherwise, the text is based on an autograph manuscript.

p. 11   Laurence Housman, *A. E. H.* (1937), p. 230.

p. 12   *Three Poems: The Parallelogram The Amphisbæna The Crocodile By A. E. Housman* (1935), pp. 7–9, slightly corrected.

p. 18   *The Elephant*: Laurence Housman, *A. E. H.*, p. 236, slightly corrected. Other versions exist: see *Poems*, ed. Burnett (1997), pp. 263, 546–7.

p. 19   *Infant Innocence*: *Memories of A. E. Housman*, by Mrs. E. W. Symons (1936), p. 4. Other versions exist: see *Poems*, ed. Burnett, pp. 263, 545–6.

p. 22   Laurence Housman, *A. E. H.*, pp. 237–8, slightly corrected.

p. 24   Laurence Housman, *A. E. H.*, p. 231.

p. 25   Typescript copy of autograph MS, slightly corrected.

p. 27   *Memories of A. E. Housman*, p. 4.

p. 30   Typescript copy of autograph MS, slightly corrected.

p. 32   *Little Miss Muffet sat on a tuffet*: *Memories of A. E. Housman*, p. 2.

p. 35   *The oyster is found in the ocean*: *Alfred Edward Housman: Recollections* by Katherine E. Symons et al. (1937), p. 27.

p. 37   Laurence Housman, *A. E. H.*, p. 58.

p. 38   *Of old the little Busy Bee*: *Alfred Edward Housman: Recollections*, pp. 24–5.

Oft when the night is chilly: ibid., pp. 27–8.